Faith on the Edge Series

S0-BYW-168

Playing God

Robert Weise

CONCORDIA PUBLISHING HOUSE · SAINT LOUIS

Written by Robert Weise

Edited by Edward Engelbrecht

This publication may be available in braille, in large print, or on cassette tape for the visually impaired. Please allow 8 to 12 weeks for delivery. Write to the Library for the Blind, 1333 S. Kirkwood Road, St. Louis, MO 63122-7295; call 1-800-433-3954, ext. 1322; or e-mail to blind.library@lcms.org.

Photo Credits: 15, 23, 37, 41, 44—BSIP Agency

3 4 5 6 7 8 9 10   11 10 09 08 07 06 05 04 03

CONTENTS

About This Series

In the past, science served as a stepchild of alchemy, a handmaiden of theology, and a tool of industry. At the beginning of the twentieth century, science took on a new role. Science became the answer to all humankind's problems. The priests and priestesses of science pulled on their white lab coats, prophesied through their theories, and consecrated each new discovery or invention. Humans marveled.

In response to these new inventions, a new type of literature arose—science fiction, which sometimes warned us about the maddening pace of technology. The robot would replace the human worker. Nuclear fallout would devastate life on earth. Science would solve people's problems by doing away with people, or at least by doing away with their humanity.

Today, people remain thankful for science. But they also recognize that science does not hold all the answers. In fact, they see that science can raise more questions than it answers, driving people on further quests for understanding, truth, and contentment.

The Faith on the Edge Bible study series tracks the progress of science and people's fascinations and fears about science. Each session introduces a contemporary topic, summarizes what science has to say about it, and then provides biblical answers and guidance so that you can face the future with the wisdom and confidence that only God can provide.

Student Introduction

Your scientists were so preoccupied with whether or not they could that they didn't stop to think whether they should.

—from the film *Jurassic Park*

At a Rotary Club presentation a few years ago, I listened in amazement to the ranting of a science fiction writer about the benefits of human cloning. Speaking from his self-created world, he joyfully anticipated the day when technology would make it possible to clone designer bodies without brains so that his brain could be transplanted into a new and youthful body whenever he needed one. When I questioned him about the ethics of such a venture, he brayed about how some people are simply too fearful to face the future and all the wonders technology can provide.

What this writer failed to understand is that it is not the technology that troubles me. It is the people who might use it, people so enthusiastic for the latest thing that they haven't considered the implications. For many tech-crazed people, "right" means getting it made and getting paid for it, and "wrong" means getting second place in the race for the future.

Though technology changes constantly, human beings don't change. The Bible records how people have always misused technology, misused their strength with fatal results. This study will help you understand the God-pleasing use of technology. It will provide you with sound guidelines and wisdom not only for this life but also for the life to come.

The Editor

CHAPTER ONE

And You'll Be Like God

Mary and John show their special parking pass to the guard. The metal gate swings open and they enter the lower-level parking area of the BioMed Plaza. As they walk to the first floor, they see a coffee shop, a floral shop, several toy and department stores, and specialty stores for prospective parents and even those who are planning their death or funeral.

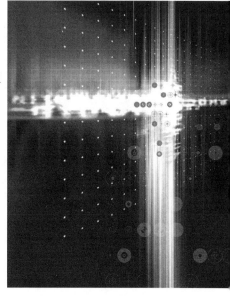

The only access to the second floor is by appointment, requiring a special identification card imprinted with their genetic code and appointment time. After they swipe their card through the genetic scanner, the elevator door opens. They enter the elevator and arrive at the second floor. Stepping out, they see the following agencies: Bundles of Love Fertility Clinic, CloneGenics, StemCell Bank, and Terminal Choices.

John says, "Biotechnology is wonderful, but is this going too far?"

Mary says, "Look at those signs. They have made-to-order babies that can be reproduced in test tubes, as well as eugenic and cloning laboratories. Why, people can even clone themselves to generate their own replacement tissues or organs." She points: "Look at that last sign, 'Terminal Choices.' It looks like a mortuary, an assisted-suicide facility, and an abortion clinic wrapped up into one."

John says, "It looks like all things are now possible."

And the serpent said to Eve, "Your eyes will be opened, and you will be like God" (Genesis 3:5).

Though the BioMed Plaza viewed by Mary and John is fictional, all the biomedical technologies it offers are available today to varying degrees.

1. Have you ever found yourself awed by modern medical procedures? By the potential that biomedical technologies offer? Give examples.

2. How might Mary and John be tempted by the BioMed Plaza in the same way that Adam and Eve were tempted by the fruit of "the tree of the knowledge of good and evil"? See Genesis 2:8–9, 15–17; 3:1–5.

3. Mary and John entered the BioMed Plaza with the best intentions. Can good intentions protect them in their medical decisions? Why or why not? See Proverbs 16:2, 25; 21:2, 30.

New Tech,
New Toys

Biomedical technology has changed humankind. These changes can be helpful or harmful. Occasionally, they may be both. Medical advances may create, sustain, alter, or destroy human life.

Biomedical technologies that *create* are referred to as Assisted Reproductive Technology (ART). A few examples of this technology are in vitro (in glass) fertilization, artificial insemination, and direct egg-sperm injection (injecting one sperm directly into one egg). The ART of in vitro fertilization may also result in the destruction of embryos during their freezing and thawing.

Biomedical technologies that *sustain* involve artificial means such as the use of respirators, feeding tubes, kidney dialysis, and pain-control therapies. When these medical technologies are abused with the intent to kill, they no longer sustain life, providing comforting, palliative care, but rather *destroy* life. Such is the case in the state of Oregon, where assisted suicide is now legal.

4. Look over the biomedical technologies mentioned in the prior two paragraphs. How common are these techniques in your community?

5. Do you know someone who has used these techniques? Did they benefit from these techniques?

Biomedical technologies that *alter* a human life are sex selection, gene replacement therapy (replacing a "bad gene" with a "good gene"), sperm and egg donation, cloning, use of spare frozen embryos for stem cell research, and organ transplants. Cloning and embryonic stem cell research will result in the *destruction* of human embryos.

6. How might these techniques alter—and possibly disrupt—human life?

Biomedical technology is an extension of our natural lives. But it is also a means to an end. The technology can be used for the common good of society; however, as suggested by the BioMed Plaza, it can also be used merely for profit or the fulfillment of personal needs and ambitions.

Biomedical therapies tend to cater to human emotions. We choose them to comfort ourselves. What we want—the human desire to improve ourselves—is apt to become the norm, the standard of right and wrong. We may feel positive about the benefits, but we are using the technology to transcend the Word of God.

7. How might emotions affect the use of biomedical techniques such as ART? Give examples.

The Tower
and the Ark

There are many biomedical technologies that serve humankind in a God-pleasing way to correct various diseases and injuries. However, we must recognize that biomedical technology can become our idol. God's Word reminds us that humans are dependent new creatures in Christ. We are not morally independent to create a "Tower of Babel." Christians struggle with the proper and improper use of biomedical technologies, especially regarding beginning- and end-of-life issues. Christians are encouraged to avoid using technology for self-serving purposes. We should approach the use of biomedical technology in service to God's Word (Colossians 3:17).

To grow in your understanding of these issues, you need to understand what God teaches about the use of technology.

8. Read Genesis 11:1–7. Why does God condemn this use of technology?

Biotechnology is a way for humans to control human life using science and nature as their instruments. This represents a shift in the stewardship of God's good gifts from "dominion" to "domination."

9. Read Genesis 6:13–16. Reflect on the use of technology described in this passage.

10. Read Genesis 2:8–9 *(AGAIN)* and 3:4–5. How do the words "playing God" fit this passage? THESE PASSAGES

11. Read and reflect on the First Commandment in Exodus 20:1–6. How does technology tend to become an "idol"?

How foolish for humankind to trample the Word of God in the rush for personal gain and greed. Self-glorification and independence are the gods of all sinners. This is Satan's playground, which leads to our isolation from God.

As persons of the trinitarian God, we have the whole Law given to us in the Ten Commandments for holy living. God wrote this Law on our hearts at creation. He gave His commands to us on two tablets of stone when He led Israel out of Egypt. Through these commands, He calls us to live as wise and loving parents, just as He is a wise and loving Father to us.

12. Read Genesis 18:19; Deuteronomy 6:5–8; and Ephesians 6:4. How might the roles and responsibilities of parenting directly conflict with the use of some reproductive therapies?

Any technology that would destroy the unborn, directly or indirectly (e.g., by freezing an embryonic human being), violates the Fifth Commandment and places our selfish desires above God who, like a dear Father, provides for us but also preserves us. As St. Paul writes: "And whatever you do, whether in word or deed, do it all in the name of the Lord Jesus, giving thanks to God the Father through Him" (Colossians 3:17). This sets apart the idolatrous motive of the builders of the Tower of Babel from that of Noah, the builder of the ark. The technologies in both cases were good and useful, but one served the self as god while the other served the triune God to His glory.

Guided by God Himself

It is very difficult to discern either the proper or improper use of biotechnology. But through prayer and meditation on the Word of God, His Spirit provides an answer (Isaiah 65:24). As baptized Christians, we are comforted in our difficult decisions because God's grace is sufficient for us in all the challenges of life (2 Corinthians 12:8–9). As you face life-and-death choices, remember the choices your heavenly Father made for you in Christ.

13. Read Ephesians 1:3–5. What choices of God does this passage describe?

14. As you face life's difficult choices, how does this passage guide and comfort you?

As redeemed Christians, we are given the eternal righteousness, innocence, and blessedness of the risen Christ. Baptized into His death and resurrection, we use and apply technology in service to the Word of God. Perhaps one of the best summaries for guidance on using technology is found in Hebrews 12.

15. Read Hebrews 12:1–3. Where does this passage direct your vision for the future? How can this passage guide and strengthen you?

16. How does your trinitarian faith, which holds to the words and promises of Jesus Christ, enable you to work through the following question regarding the use and abuse of biotechnology: "Where does a Christian draw the line?"

Words to Remember

A nd whatever you do, whether in word or deed, do it all in the name of the Lord Jesus, giving thanks to God the Father through Him. Colossians 3:17

CHAPTER TWO

In the Beginning God Created

B ob and I received our referral to Bundles of Love Fertility Clinic at the BioMed Plaza. Dr. Smith, the director, met us at the door and took us to his office.

Since my husband and I each carry the gene for cystic fibrosis, we were referred to Dr. Smith's clinic for in vitro fertilization. The main purpose of this referral was to test all our in-vitro-produced embryos for the cystic fibrosis gene. The test is called "preimplantation genetic testing." If an embryo contains a cystic fibrosis gene from each of us, the embryo will develop into a child with cystic fibrosis. Dr. Smith explained that all embryos carrying the disease (one gene contributed by one parent) or exhibiting the disease (one gene contributed by each parent) would be destroyed. Only the disease-free embryos would be placed into my womb.

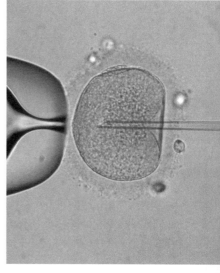

I commented to Dr. Smith, "Right now, my husband and I feel all right with this because embryos really aren't human beings. They don't have arms, legs, or a beating heart. They aren't aware of their surroundings. An embryo is no more than a blob of cells."

As we left the BioMed Plaza, Bob said, "Joan, I'm not sure about this. Is that tiny embryo just a 'blob of cells,' or is it truly a human being? What about our faith? Are we in danger of playing God by choosing which embryos will live and which will die?"

As we reached the car, Bob recalled a few words from the Bible quoted in a pro-life Sunday sermon: "When I was woven together in the depths of the earth, Your eyes saw my unformed body" (Psalm 139:15b–16a).

17. Relate Joan's description of the unborn child as a "blob of cells" to the practice of abortion. Compare this to King David's description of the unborn in Psalm 139:13–16.

18. How might Bob and Joan rationalize or justify a decision to reject an embryo with the gene for cystic fibrosis?

Defining Life

19. Is a human-procreated zygote (a unicellular embryo) a human being with potential or a potential human being?

M any scientists believe that an embryo doesn't have the same moral status as a newborn or infant because it lacks the possibility of *sentience* (being aware of its surroundings). Also, they point out that each cell within the embryo hasn't "decided" what it will form. Lastly, the high rate of natural mortality of embryos within the womb assures these scientists that they are simply following the example of nature by choosing which embryo will live.

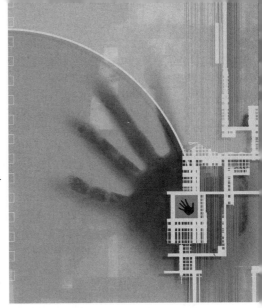

Some pro-choice organizations and many politicians believe that a human being's life begins at implantation (a period of about six days after fertilization, when the embryo attaches to the wall of the uterus).

20. Even though single-celled organisms like amoebas are very small, scientists regard them as living beings. Why might they classify an embryo differently?

Some embryologists (experts in the process of natal human development) have argued that each human being begins at fertilization, when the genetic material from the woman's egg and the man's sperm are united. The process of development continues in the uterus until birth. Hence, conception and in utero development are part of a continuing process that has a specific purpose: birth.

21. Summarize how science confirms that at fertilization the genetic union of sperm and egg causes procreation (a new human life).

17

Doctors usually divide human development into two periods: prenatal (before birth) and postnatal (after birth). According to embryologist Keith Moore, birth is merely a dramatic event *during* development, resulting in a change in environment. Development does not stop at birth. According to Dr. Jim Russell, the brain does not complete its neurological development until around the age of 30!

As Dr. Diane Irving points out, scientists know when human life begins; the question is when does the life of a *human being* begin. Since all body cells are given human life by the Lord God Creator, the correct scientific language for the developing in utero human is a human being, *not* merely human life.

22. Why are the terms *human being* and *human life* important? How do they differ?

A human being has a body and a soul. In the most simplistic language, a human wife and a human husband procreate according to God's will, creating another human life of equal value and dignity. This is a scientific and theological fact. It is also the moral basis for our life together as humans.

God Defines Life

Some scientists define the moral status of a human being based on possession or lack of possession of certain "rational attributes," such as sentience, or "biological attributes," such as a nervous system. This establishes identity on the basis of what a human being has and not on the basis of what a human being has been given by God in Christ at conception. Attempting to define the beginning of a human's life on the basis of rational or biological attributes or location (in the womb or out of the womb) is arbitrary.

For example, according to the National Institute of Health, the Human Embryo Research Panel of 1994 reported that the embryo is not a human being because it is not aware of its surroundings (i.e., nonsentient). However, readers should recognize that sentience is ill-defined. It is a philosophical concept that has been imposed on the scientific data. Since the lack of sentience qualifies an embryo as a nonhuman being, some scientists use this as permission to experiment on an embryo or destroy it.

23. How might the sentience rule affect the following groups of people: the mentally ill, the severely mentally retarded, Alzheimer's patients, and the permanently unconscious?

The arbitrary and capricious character of the rules about sentience and development show themselves through another example: the mortality rate of embryos. Some scientists argue that the high rate of natural mortality of embryos in the uterus (approximately 30 to 70 percent) demonstrates that the embryo is a nonhuman being because it dies before implantation. Since when does death define whether someone is a human being? What percentage of human adults die? 100 percent! (with a few miraculous exceptions recorded in the Bible). Does that mean human adults aren't human beings?

24. What are some problems with defining humans based on death? Read Romans 5:12.

If the embryo is viewed as a nonhuman being, scientists are permitted to use it as they wish—the end justifies the means if a "nonhuman" is destroyed. However, the Law of God speaks clearly: "You shall not murder." We are "neighbor" to the embryonic human being (Luke 10:36–37).

If you consider an embryo a human being, then you will be guided by that belief. If you consider it to be only a potential human being, then you will be guided by that belief. Whatever your idea is about the moral status of the embryonic human being, you will find yourself basing your decisions on that idea. But what does God think?

The Lord said to Jeremiah, "Before I formed you in the womb I knew you, before you were born I set you apart" (Jeremiah 1:5). Some say that this is a special case that cannot be applied to human conception in the present-day world. Yet the Scriptures testify in other places that God knew us before the foundations of the world were created (Ephesians 1:4).

25. Read Psalm 139:13–16. Reflect on its meaning for defining human beings and life.

Another important passage assisting the Christian in understanding that the unborn are human beings is found in Exodus 21.

26. Read Exodus 21:22–23. How does this law view the life in the womb?

The Hebrew word for "child" is *yeled*. Other passages that use this term give us greater understanding of how the biblical authors viewed life. For example, in Genesis 21:15, Ishmael was at least 14 years old when the Scriptures referred to him as a *boy*. In Genesis 37:2, Joseph was at least 17 years old when he was referred to as a *young man*. In 2 Chronicles 10:8, 10, 14, Rehoboam began his rule over Judah at the age of 41 (2 Chronicles 12:13). Before his reign, he rejected the counsel of the elders and received advice from *young men* described as Rehoboam's contemporaries and peers. The same Hebrew word—*yeled*—is used for all these ages. This suggests that regardless of the stage of development of an individual, the biblical authors and the Lord who inspired them view that individual as a human being, a person.

27. Based on the above passages, how might you answer people who use development as the basis for deciding when an embryo/fetus is a human being?

28. Look up Isaiah 7:14; Luke 1:31, 41, 57; 2:6–7. According to these passages, how does the Bible describe what is in the womb?

29. What conclusion can you draw from these terms?

Made Man

One of the most profound testimonies that the unborn are human beings is learned from the incarnation: God taking on the flesh of a human being in the person of Jesus Christ, God's only begotten Son. The second person of the Trinity was "made in human likeness" (Philippians 2:7).

30. Read Hebrews 2:17. Why was Jesus born?

When the early Christians summarized what the Bible teaches about who Jesus is, they stated that He was "conceived by the Holy Spirit of the virgin Mary and made man" (Nicene Creed).

31. According to the early Christians, when did Jesus become a human being? What made Jesus a man?

32. Read 1 Timothy 2:5; Luke 24:39; and Matthew 26:38. Why does the Bible emphasize this aspect of Jesus' person? What comfort do these passages provide you? In view of these passages, what makes a human being?

Words
to Remember

By Him all things were created: things in heaven and on earth, visible and invisible. Colossians 1:16

CHAPTER THREE

In Search of the Perfect Child

Joe and Sue received their special pass by registered mail for the Bundles of Love Fertility Clinic at the BioMed Plaza. As they stepped from the elevator, Doctor Love greeted them warmly and led them to his office. Joe and Sue sat with him and explained their desire to have a "normal" child, that is, one who would be free from any genetic disorder. The doctor assured them that their needs would be met.

Joe said, "We have been unable to have a child through normal sexual means for the past several years. Sue has been told that her eggs are not good enough for fertilization. We will have to seek a child through egg donation."

Dr. Love said, "We can help you select, in a very general way—weight, IQ, hair color, athletic ability, blood type, eye color—the child of your choice through our egg donation computer catalog. We can usually determine gender by selecting from your husband's sperm one that will produce a girl or one that will produce a boy. The former is 95 percent successful, while the latter is 75 percent successful."

"Wow!" Sue said. "That means we can plan the decor of the nursery ahead of time."

"You can really determine the baby's

hair color?" Joe asked.

"Remember," Dr. Love said, "choosing characteristics of your child is nonspecific. We can only get you in the ballpark."

"By the way," Sue asked, "what is the average cost for one in vitro cycle for making our baby?"

"The average cost for one IVF cycle is about $67,000, as published in the *New England Journal of Medicine*," Dr. Love said. "It could be more and it could be less. Since we have to go to an egg donor, that additional cost will depend on the education, IQ, and professional level of that donor. In some cases, the undergraduate academic institution that she graduated from may be important and, perhaps, add to your cost. The range is $3,000 to $10,000. Sex selection will cost about $2,000 to $3,000. Will any of this be a problem?"

"Nothing's too good for our baby," the couple said in unison.

Dr. Love said, "In addition, a legal agreement will have to be drawn up to assure that you own any spare embryos, since the egg donor is the biological mother of the child that you will bear in your womb."

As Joe and Sue were leaving the BioMed Plaza, Joe seemed troubled by all of this. He said, "While we were sitting there, I thought to myself that we Christians should be content in anything and everything. Are we trying to satisfy ourselves by searching for the perfect child? Should we just trust in the Lord and try not to control so much? Is this 'making' a child or is this 'begetting' a child like the Bible describes? The barrenness issue is very tough to deal with in the face of all of this Assisted Reproductive Technology."

Fertility

The following paragraphs about ART are not meant to judge the situations in which it is used appropriately or inappropriately nor to bind the Christian's conscience. This section is about getting the facts straight.

Infertility is defined as the inability of a married couple to conceive and bear a child after one year of unprotected sexual relations. About 10–15 percent of all married couples are infertile. Approximately 35–40 percent of infertility issues are related to females and the same percentage to males. Approximately 20 percent of infertility issues are related to both husband and wife, while a very small percentage of couples are infertile for unexplained reasons.

33. Read Genesis 30:1–24. Discuss the emotional and personal aspects of infertility.

A couple today may choose to conceive and bear a child through several artificial methods. A child may be artificially conceived either within the woman's body or outside her body. There are two main reproductive procedures that may create a child within the woman's body. The first is called artificial insemination (AI). This medical procedure requires the recovery of male sperm from the husband, placing them directly into the woman's reproductive tract. The second artificial method of conceiving a child within the woman's womb is called gamete intrafallopian transfer (GIFT). Herein, a concentration of sperm and usually no more than three eggs are injected together into the upper end of the woman's fallopian tube with the intent that fertilization will occur at that location.

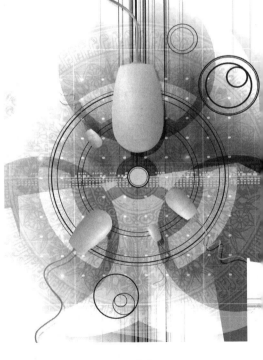

The most commonly used artificial method of making a baby outside the woman's body is called in vitro fertilization (IVF; *in vitro* means "in glass"). Direct egg sperm injection (DESI) is less frequently used. In the former process, male sperm and female eggs are removed and cleaned. Usually 6 to 35 eggs are recovered from a woman. Millions of sperm may be removed from the man. Using the man's sperm, the woman's eggs are fertilized in a petri dish. In general, no more than three fertilized eggs are placed into the woman's uterus at one time. If there are spare embryos, they are frozen in liquid nitrogen at about -321° F. The second artificial procedure, direct egg sperm injection, involves the isolation of one sperm, which is injected directly into the woman's egg in a petri dish. The resultant zygote is placed into the woman's womb. In all of the artificial procedures described, a couple may also choose to use donated sperm, donated eggs, and a donated womb (called a surrogate womb).

34. Read Genesis 2:22–25; Exodus 20:15; and Leviticus 18:4–6. How would these biblical guidelines help you determine whether making a baby in a petri dish accords with God's will?

Legal agreements are also frequently drawn up to address the issue of frozen spare embryos. Couples must decide in advance who will have custody of these frozen embryos in the case of death or divorce. In addition, if a sibling or other relative donates her eggs to her sister, a legal agreement must be drawn up to decide who has custody over any spare embryos, since the donating sister or relative is the biological mother. The same approach would apply for sperm donation, since the donor would be the biological father.

35. Reflect on the legal agreements involved in the use of fertility technology. What makes these agreements necessary? What do these agreements imply about the life potential of the eggs and sperm involved?

In some cases of surrogacy, elective abortion clauses are added. In the laboratory setting, sperm, eggs, and the resultant embryos created in the petri dish are graded regarding their ability to either fertilize or implant. Only those embryos that look viable to the "naked eye" are kept for implantation or freezing.

36. Read Genesis 16:1–6. What does the biblical story of Abraham, Sarah, and Hagar teach you about the use of a surrogate womb? What does it teach you about a childless couple's desire to have a child of their own?

37. If a sister decides to donate her eggs to her sister and brother-in-law, how would you respond to their motive: "God teaches us that this is the loving and caring thing to do"?

Be Fruitful

The Lord God brought man and woman together as one-flesh, sexual beings. Before and since the fall of Adam and Eve into sin, the Lord's command to Adam and Eve (which includes all humankind) has been to be fruitful and multiply (Genesis 1:28; 9:1). This is procreation, commonly known in the Bible as "begetting." A married couple's primary intention as one flesh is their sexual union, their mutual love, and if it is God's will, the procreation of a child.

Oliver O'Donovan writes that the biblical term *beget* describes our ability to procreate another human being, not by our power of will or intention but because of who we are. The creation of a child outside the mutual sexual embrace described in the Bible separates the one-flesh union from the intentional act of sexual intercourse and places it within the context of the laboratory.

Couples must guard against violating the First, Fifth, Ninth, and

Tenth Commandments. When the quest to have a child becomes an obsession for self-fulfillment, the First Commandment is violated. If embryos are frozen, couples need to know that 30–70 percent die in the thawing process. This violates the Fifth Commandment. If sperm and egg are received via donation, then the Ninth and Tenth Commandments are violated. Some theologians would include the Sixth Commandment about adultery (remember the custody agreements necessary for these procedures!). In addition, this quest for a child by any means violates the one-flesh union and the marriage vows to remain faithful to God's Word and to each other until death.

Some Assisted Reproductive Technology, such as artificial insemination, seems to be within the one-flesh union, as the child is conceived within the reproductive system of the wife. Other types of ART that make a child outside the body of the husband and the wife are subject to idolatrous abuse. In these cases, the married couple tends to be "producers" of a child. Their embryos are rated according to viability; spare embryos are frozen, which may cause their premature death; thawing of spare embryos often causes death; the financial cost of making a baby outside the womb may drive the husband and wife apart; and lastly, their parenting is based on personal control and fulfillment.

38. In light of the death and resurrection of Jesus Christ, how would you respond to the questions posed by the couple in the story about the BioMed Plaza at the beginning of this chapter (p. 23)?

Content in Christ

Following the original sin of Adam and Eve, barrenness became a terrible stigma and emotional trauma. Over the centuries, this has not changed. However, the Lord never condemns those who are barren, but rather brings them comfort and consolation through His

Gospel of mercy and compassion. Some stories of barrenness in the Bible are the following: Abram and Sarai (Genesis 15:4; 16:1–2); Rebekah (Genesis 25:20–21); Rachel and Leah (Genesis 29:31–30:24); Abimelech's wife and female slaves (Genesis 20:17–18); Manoah's wife (Judges 13:1–24); and Hannah (1 Samuel 1:1–20).

39. Desire and determination can be great strengths. How does God's will and desire come to fulfillment in the story of Abram and Sarai?

Infertile couples are encouraged to search the Scriptures, praying and learning all that they can about making a child outside the one-flesh union. The emotional trauma of barren couples needs attention from all members of the body of Christ (1 Corinthians 12:12–26). Remember, the love of God in Christ "does no harm to its neighbor" (Romans 13:10), which includes the unborn.

In this life, perfection is a laudable yet ever-unattainable goal. That's because each of us derives from the flawed raw material of sinful men and women—each of us except Christ. Jesus was conceived by the Holy Spirit. Though He partook of His mother's human nature, He did not inherit her sin. As the Son of God, He was the perfect child, entrusted to us so that we, through Him, might again trust the perfect love and forgiveness of our heavenly Father.

40. Read Philippians 3:4b–14. What perfection does the apostle seek apart from his bloodline and good behavior? How does he seek it?

The trinitarian faith of barren couples holds to the resurrected Christ and His promises. Jesus knows the desires and emotional trauma that infertility generates. Since the Word of God does not address the specific use of Assisted Reproductive Technology, couples are encouraged to examine their motives for making a child through the cross and resurrection of Jesus Christ.

The Lord Jesus Christ is the Author and Creator of all life, especially a human being's life. He died so that those who are created in the mutual sexual love of a husband and wife would be baptized and raised in the instruction and discipline of the Lord (Ephesians 6:1–3). Hence, through the love of God in Christ Jesus, Christian couples that are barren receive wholeness through the resurrected Christ.

The couple that is childless has a child, for the Child that was conceived by the Holy Spirit and born of the Virgin Mary is born for them. In Him infertile couples have their being and their life. In Christ, all couples, whether barren or fruitful, live first and always the life of Christ in the world.

41. Read Philippians 3:10–11. Is the wholeness of God's people received in Christ without heartache? Explain.

Words
to Remember

Knowledge puffs up, but love builds up. The man who thinks he knows something does not yet know as he ought to know. But the man who loves God is known by God. 1 Corinthians 8:1–3

CHAPTER FOUR

The Immortal Clone

Mr. and Mrs. Johnson arrive at the BioMed Plaza for their appointment at CloneGenics, Inc. Their 7-year-old daughter was killed recently by a drunk driver while she was riding her bicycle. The doctor assures them that he can clone their daughter, but that she will probably have a different personality, interests, and hobbies. Other than similarity in looks, the clone will be a different person. The Johnsons don't care.

Before the cloning process begins, the Johnsons agree to undergo a psychiatric evaluation and genetic profile. If they are approved, their "daughter" will be cloned. Three cloned embryos will be implanted in a surrogate womb. The Johnsons agree to pay $200,000 to cover the procedure, healthcare costs, and legal agreements. Everything has been approved. It's a go!

As the Johnsons leave the BioMed Plaza, they discuss their office visit. Mrs. Johnson turns to her husband and says, "Will this really be our child or merely a younger twin of our daughter? And how will this cloned child deal with the fact that she is a replacement?"

Mr. Johnson says, "I recall hearing our pastor say, regarding the use of cloning technology, 'Everything is permissible—but not everything is beneficial. Everything is permissible—but not everything is constructive. Nobody should seek his own good, but the good of others.' Are we being masters of our life or servants to God's Word?"

42. What difficulties might the Johnsons face in their effort to get back their daughter?

43. Answer their question, "Are we being masters of our life or servants to God's Word?" Support your answer.

Making Copies

44. Based on what you've read in the news or other sources, what is cloning?

According to *Stedman's Concise Medical Dictionary,* human cloning means transplanting the chromosomes from a human cell into a human egg from which the genetic material has already been removed. You don't clone a person. You clone a person's genetic material, the DNA that is responsible for a person's physical looks.

It is important to review the prevalent cloning method: (1) an egg is removed from a woman; (2) the nucleus containing the woman's genetic material is removed without damaging the egg; (3) a somatic cell, such as a skin cell, is removed from the person being cloned; (4) this cell is set aside so that it becomes inactivated, that is, it no longer "recognizes itself" as a specialized somatic cell, but just as a cell with 46 chromosomes containing the sex chromosomes, either an XX if a woman is going to be cloned or an XY if a man is going to be cloned; (5) the inactivated somatic cell is brought in contact with the cell membrane of the anucleated egg (without a nuclear DNA), after which a slight electrical charge is applied, causing the body cell to fuse with the egg cell; (6) the 46 chromosomes enter the egg, causing the egg to "think" that it is a zygote or fertilized egg; (7) this cloned zygote is placed in a surrogate womb so that in 38–42 weeks either a clone female or male is born.

The resulting human clone may be compared to an identical twin of the person from whom he/she is cloned. While a clone may look like the person from whom it is cloned, it will be different in its behavioral and social skills.

45. Some people have wondered whether a clone will be a human being and have a soul. What do you think?

Consider the following case: A husband and wife decide to use cloning technology to have a "child" that will come from the husband's cells. The husband is 35 years old; this means the husband will essentially be 35 years older than his cloned "twin."

46. What false expectations might a person have about cloning?

Some families will seek to use this technology to "resurrect" their domestic pet. Some scientists are already using cloning technology to save endangered animal species such as the bald eagle, the Bengal tiger, and the like. The company that assisted in the cloning of the first cat, called Copy Cat (C.C.), is Genetics Savings and Clone.

Parenting

C onsider this scenario: Marion is sitting on a bed holding a photograph of her lost son whom she hopes to replace with human cloning technology. She has had a few inches of his somatic skin cells preserved in liquid nitrogen so that when the cloning technology is perfected, she will be able to bring him back, at least in terms of his looks.

47. Reflect on Marion's wishes and her plan.

Christians must return to the basics of what we should do, what we shouldn't do, and how we are to live the life of Christ in the world. The Lord established marriage as a one-flesh union, husband and wife. If it is God's will, a couple may be blessed with a child through sexual procreation or adoption. Viewing cloning from the doctrine of marriage and parenting, the cloning of "self," that is, the husband or wife, violates the Word of God, especially the Ninth and Tenth Commandments about coveting. Of course, when these commandments are violated, then they all are broken, since God is the author of them all (James 2:8–11).

48. Read James 2:8–11. What happens to the Law when one part gets broken?

The "producing" mentality of cloning is seeking to control destiny and turn procreation into an industry. This mentality also gives way to eugenics. *Eugenics* is crass social hygiene. It strives to mate the "best" humans. All other people are eventually eliminated. In this way, only good, productive individuals in society are reproduced, assuring that the best genetic characteristics will be passed on from generation to generation.

49. Eugenics, by its very nature, emphasizes human prejudice and creates classes of human beings. As a result, it brings into question the rights or even the humanness of those who lack the proper genetic makeup. What result has eugenics produced in the past?

Eugenics is with us already through Assisted Reproductive Technology. For example, sperm donated by Nobel laureates, Ivy League school graduates, and others with high IQs and other special academic or athletic abilities are available for a significant fee. This approach to procreation exchanges the natural for the unnatural, that is, the sexual one-flesh union for the asexual reproduction of "self." The cloning of "self" exacerbates the move away from the biblical world of the one-flesh union and procreation as God's work to child manufacturing and production.

50. How might the effort to make better people through eugenics actually lead to a lack of respect for human life?

The most sinful god is the god of self. Satan tempts Christians by emphasizing that cloning would bring fulfillment of the Lord's command to "be fruitful and multiply." Satan may tempt us to use this technology to escape the pain of infertility, to replace a dead loved one, or to create youthful spare body parts. But even the youngest legs cannot outrun the accusations of God's Law.

51. Is perfection of human life possible? Why or why not? Read Romans 3:23.

52. Read 1 Samuel 17:4–7 and 1 Kings 11:4–6. Does stronger, faster, or smarter necessarily make a better person? Why or why not?

53. In light of the biblical teaching about marriage and procreation, how does cloning invite infertile couples or those who seek to replace a deceased loved one to adopt a "producer" attitude towards children?

Your Eternal Family

C hristians are saved by grace through faith (Ephesians 2:8). Through the death, resurrection, and ascension of the Lord Jesus Christ, we have been saved from sin, death, and the power of the devil. Having baptized us into Christ's death and resurrection, God enables us to have no other gods before Him. We belong to God. He is responsible for us and promises us greater blessings than this life could ever promise.

54. Read 1 Corinthians 15:42–49. Contrast the "promise" of cloning with God's promises here.

55. Read 1 Thessalonians 4:13–18. How does this passage provide genuine comfort?

Christians respond by faith to His good gifts of creation, redemption, and sanctification. Sin distorts and compromises this relationship. By the grace of God, Christians are called to remain faithful and true to the Word of God that is given to us through the Author and Perfecter of our faith (Hebrews 12:1–3). Cloning technology is not true to the Word of God regarding procreation and parenting. It creates a Tower of Babel syndrome that Satan uses to separate and isolate a married couple from their marriage vows, from each other, and from their Redeemer.

Marriage is a gift given by the Lord God. Procreation of a child is a gift given by the Lord God. By His grace, married couples who struggle with infertility will "fear, love and trust in God above all things." While it is sometimes difficult to know which Assisted Reproductive Technologies can be used to the glory of God and in service to His Word, cloning technology clearly violates the one-flesh union and parenting commands given by the Lord God. As baptized children of God, we never face the frustrations and disappointments of life alone. Our heavenly Father knows our troubles and agonies. He walks with us, promising to never leave us or forsake us.

Words to Remember

"Everything is permissible for me"—but not everything is beneficial. "Everything is permissible for me"—but I will not be mastered by anything. 1 Corinthians 6:12

CHAPTER FIVE

The Stem Cell Revolution

My father suffers from Parkinson's disease. His name is Teddy. Teddy's geriatrician and neurologist referred him to the BioMed Plaza StemCell Bank. The bank specializes in growing tissues and organs from spare frozen or cloned human embryos and in growing adult stem cells from umbilical cords and placentas. Unused embryos from Bundles of Love Fertility Clinic and those created at CloneGenics are frozen and kept for those couples who want embryonic stem cell tissue and organ production to cover the future possibility of tissue or organ transplantation.

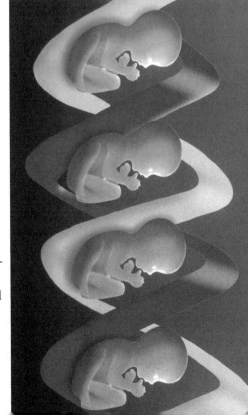

After we arrive at StemCell Bank, they wheel Teddy to their laboratory for blood evaluation to determine what spare frozen embryonic stem cells will be compatible with his body. They don't find a compatible match. To avoid this rejection problem, Teddy will undergo "therapeutic cloning." They will create embryos that have been cloned from his skin cells. In essence, they are cloning my father to save him or, at least, to buy him some time.

Teddy's five-day-old cloned embryos will be destroyed to remove and isolate dopamine-producing nerve cells. These isolated cells will be injected into his brain to treat his Parkinson's disease, especially those terrible tremors. An appointment is set up for the surgical transplantation of the dopamine-producing stem cells into a specific area of his brain. It will take place in two weeks, but Teddy will have to wait about eight to twelve weeks to see if he receives some relief or a cure from the tremors.

Leaving the BioMed Plaza, I recall the words of a hospital chaplain who expressed his reservations regarding the use of this biotechnology: "Do you not know that your body is a temple of the Holy Spirit, who is in you, whom you have received from God? You are not your own; you were bought at a price. Therefore, honor God with your body" (1 Corinthians 6:19–20).

Such Great Potential

56. Briefly share what you know about the debate over stem cell research.

Stem cells are cells that have the ability to divide indefinitely, giving rise to specific cells or tissues such as those for the kidney, heart, bone marrow, muscles, and so on. There are two sources for stem cells. Adult stem cells (ASC) are found in the adult organism (e.g., in the bone marrow, skin, intestine, umbilical cords, placenta). These ASC replenish tissues in which cells often have limited life spans. Embryonic stem cells (ESC) are derived from the inner cell mass of a four- or five-day-old human embryo/blastocyst.

ASC are taken from consenting adults and do not involve the destruction of an embryonic human being. ESC involves the destruc-

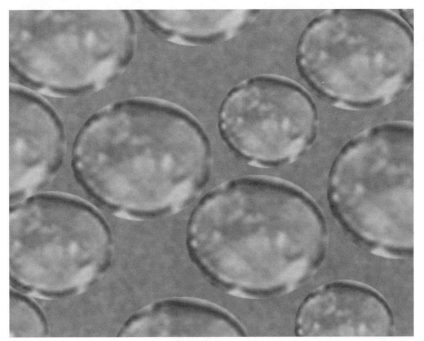

tion of an embryonic human being who is unable to give its consent. This is a violation of the Nuremberg Code.

57. Some ethicists believe that exercising the will determines what is good (pro-choice). How does cloning violate this pro-choice principle?

While ASC can be taken from consenting adults, ESC acquisition requires two processes involving embryonic human beings. First, ESC may be recovered from embryos that have been created by in vitro fertilization and then frozen. These frozen embryos are either abandoned or made available for donation by their parents.

A second possible origin of ESC is through a process called therapeutic cloning. This uses the same process of cloning described in the last session. This process is performed to eliminate organ and tissue rejection (since you would be cloning your own DNA), but also uses a developing embryo called a blastocyst.

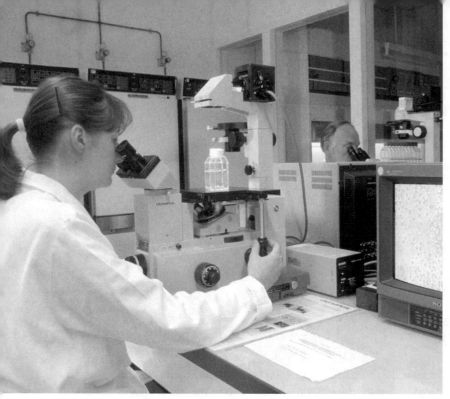

58. Consider the following scenario: Company A makes cloned cells, then sells them to company B to take them apart and use for therapeutic purposes. How might buying and selling affect moral choices at these companies?

Therapeutic cloning is being promoted over and against reproductive cloning. The scientific process is the same in both technologies, with one major difference: therapeutic cloning destroys the embryonic human being at about the fifth day to recover stem cells, whereas reproductive cloning allows for the complete gestational development of the cloned human being. Since society has trouble with the idea of making clones but less trouble with destroying embryos, scientists and politicians promote therapeutic cloning. Since the embryo in both cases isn't considered to be a human being, killing it makes little difference to those involved in this research.

Life or Tool?

C hristians justified by God (Romans 5:1) are called to holy living. The Ten Commandments serve as our guide to holy living. In addition, we have learned from the Scriptures that an embryo is a human being, endowed with a body and a soul. Therefore, people who seek to clone themselves to produce cells or tissues for therapeutic purposes forget that this does not honor God with their bodies (1 Corinthians 6:20). Let's take a closer look at these principles.

Deliberate destruction awaits embryonic human beings created for their stem cells. Such destruction also awaits spare frozen embryos created and then abandoned by infertile couples.

59. What is another way to say "deliberate destruction" when talking about a human being?

60. In what ways does the use of cloning technology to alleviate Teddy's tremors (p. 41) violate God's Word?

61. How would you respond to a person who says, "God gave us the technical ability to clone. Shouldn't we use that ability?"

62. React to the following statement: "If you lose the honor and respect for the embryonic human being's life, you will lose the honor and respect for all human beings, regardless of their age and developmental stage."

Depend
on the Lord

C hristians are dependent and not independent human beings. God in Christ brings us into a covenant relationship through Holy Baptism and the pure Gospel of Jesus Christ. This places a Christian not only in a relationship with the Lord God, but also with the body of Christ, the holy Christian church on earth, the communion of saints.

63. Beginning with conception, reflect on how God has made dependence a constant aspect of human life.

Christians need to see the use of medical technology to help correct or care for a debilitating physical ailment in view of their birth into a human family and Baptism into the communion of saints. The wanton destruction of spare human embryos or their creation via cloning and subsequent destruction turns this dependent covenant relationship into an independent, self-serving relationship.

God's care for us in Christ enables us to care for all human beings, regardless of their location or developmental status. Human life, its creation, redemption, and sanctification, are blessed gifts from

the Lord Jesus Christ. Living the life of Christ within this covenant calls into question any biotechnology that causes humankind to make independence their destiny.

64. Paul's letter to the Galatians describes a situation where people sought salvation through a customary medical procedure. Where does Paul tell the Galatians they will find true independence? Read Galatians 5:1–6.

Before God, frozen and created embryos have a living purpose—to be His own and live with Him in His eternal kingdom forever. Christians view the sanctity of a human being's life through the cross of Jesus Christ. The cross says that Yahweh is in control. By His Holy Spirit, we are enabled to fear and trust in God above the use of technology that may lead us into the sin of idolatry through cloning and petri-dish abortions of embryonic human beings.

65. Read Galatians 5:13–14. How did Christ win freedom for you?

God is the Author and Creator of human life. His agape love, given to us in Christ, bears, believes, hopes, and endures all things. This love never fails.

66. How does the cross of Christ assist Christians to see through the temptation of correcting Parkinson's disease, Alzheimer's disease, and spinal cord injuries through cloning technologies?

Words
to Remember

Do you not know that your body is the temple of the Holy Spirit who is in you, whom you have received from God? You are not your own; you were bought at a price. Therefore, honor God with your body. 1 Corinthians 6:19–20

CHAPTER SIX

The Valley of the Shadow of Death

My father, Bob, is suffering from Lou Gehrig's disease. My mother died two years ago from complications arising from Alzheimer's disease. Bob is fully competent; however, he is in the end stage of this disease, which causes him to lose control of all of the muscles in his body. A ventilator breathes for him. A feeding tube nourishes him. He receives morphine to manage his discomfort. He could be kept alive for several months, perhaps several years. At least he's able to live at home.

However, as a result of his increasing muscular weakness and general wasting, he has decided that life is not worth living. Bob doesn't want the disease to "get" him. He wants to die on his own terms. Therefore, he is contemplating a visit to Terminal

49

Choices at the BioMed Plaza for information about their assisted suicide program. He's thinking about asking his physician to turn his ventilator off. He also wishes to donate all of his usable organs so that others may benefit from his death.

Even though he has a Durable Power of Attorney for Health Care (proxy directive) and a Do Not Resuscitate order, our family is divided over what he wants to do. As my family and I gather together with our father to discuss what should be done, I recall a few words from my pastor: "If we live, we live to the Lord; and if we die, we die to the Lord. So, whether we live or die, we belong to the Lord" (Romans 14:8).

67. Apply the pastor's words to Bob's situation.

68. What help can a Durable Power of Attorney offer to a Christian family?

The New Face
of Death

A few decades ago, when a person was dying at home, at a hospital, or at a care center, he or she was surrounded by loved ones. Much of our current technology and health care directives were not in common use. Medicine was primarily low tech, with a majority of sick people dying quickly of acute illness. According to Dr. Robert D. Orr of the Christian Medical Dental Society, 90 percent of North Americans today die slowly from debilitating disease (organ failure, malignancy, dementia, etc.). Because of the use of high-tech interventions and because families are often unavailable to care for dying relatives at home, 74 percent of people die in institutions.

69. Does technology always improve people's lives? Explain.

At the end of life, care is emphasized over cure, and being a servant over being a "fixer." Pain management is given a top priority in patient comfort care. Yet sometimes pastors or family members fear giving too much pain medication. They fear that such pain medication could suppress the patient's breathing, with possibly fatal results.

Family members and pastors must learn about the "principle of double effect." The good effects of pain drugs outweigh the risks of their effects on respiration, blood pressure, pulse, and heart rate. According to Dr. Orr, concern about respiratory suppression from narcotics is greatly exaggerated. Pain stimulates breathing above normal, causing rapid, shallow breaths. The application of pain drugs brings a person's respiration back to a comfortable level. Breathing is normal (15–20 breaths per minute) and deeper when pain is managed appropriately. Managing pain is not an "all or nothing" approach. The good effect—managing pain with the careful application of narcotics —outweighs the bad effect of respiratory suppression.

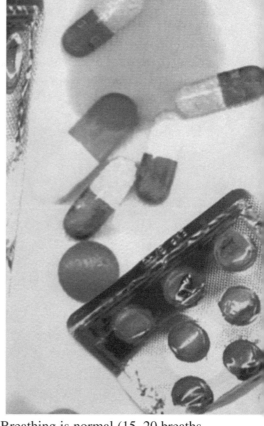

70. How likely is it that your family will face a life-and-death decision about palliative care? What more do you need to know about end of life issues?

Though it is often very difficult to predict when a patient will die, it usually becomes clear when he or she is "dying" (e.g., organs are shutting down, increased weakness is observed with a decrease in oral intake, rapid pulse, cold and mottled extremities). A family's anxieties over observing the dying process can be lessened by (1) their presence, (2) medical explanation that all these symptoms are normal, and (3) the presence of an experienced caregiver such as a nurse, pastor, or chaplain.

71. Dr. Gilbert Meilaender has said that the refusal of treatment doesn't mean the refusal of life. What do you think he means?

72. When might people think of death as a solution? Read 1 Corinthians 15:20–26 and reflect on how Paul describes death.

Unnatural Death

Secular views of dying and death, especially suffering at the end of life, are strangely contradictory. For example, many secular thinkers view death as the ultimate terror that must be avoided at all costs by the exaggerated use of medical treatments that are doomed to fail. Others, however, may view a human being's life as so broken and the quality of life as so pathetically poor that such life isn't worth living.

Sin gives people the false impression that they are in control of their living and their dying. Many think of death as simply a part of living. Satan may use two other secular doctrines to make them complacent about death: (1) the principle of utilitarianism, that is, seeking the greatest good for the greatest number of people, and (2) the theory of natural Darwinism.

Both of these views lead to the sin of idolatry and ultimately deny that we are finite, sinful human beings whose physical death is not natural. Both ideas can be used to justify keeping a person alive at all costs (even though the art of medicine says that the treatment is useless and excessively burdensome) or to end a person's life via euthanasia or assisted suicide.

In contrast to these ideas, Dr. Joel Okomoto says: "God is God" (Exodus 3:14). God forbids us to take the life of another person (murder, abortion, euthanasia) or our own life (suicide or assisted suicide). He assures us that He is in control. He is the one whom we should fear, love, and trust above all things.

73. Read Deuteronomy 32:39. What does the Lord proclaim in this text? What does this mean for your life?

We are to always care for those who are ill and at the end of their earthly life. We are called to be kind and compassionate to one another, to forgive one another, and especially to bear one another's burdens. The Word of the Lord God declares this to be meet, right, and beneficial for Christians living the life of Christ in the world.

Alive
in Christ

The Lord God creates a human being's life. In the beginning He made our first parents by His Word, and we human beings were perfectly made. But our bodies and souls are now corrupted by sin.

God is God. His Son, Jesus Christ, the Savior of all humankind, has restored to us His perfect love and righteousness by His grace through faith. For daily bread, life, and breath, we depend on Him. He takes responsibility for us, caring for us through His means of grace, the Gospel, Holy Baptism, and the Lord's Supper.

74. Read Revelation 4:11. Why did God make you?

Healing for the sick and dying begins with repentance and faith, knowing that in our suffering, God in Christ forgives our sins by faith alone. Hence, we go to the cross of Jesus Christ not to learn how to deal with suffering at the end of life, but to know that by faith alone our suffering is not in vain.

75. Read Romans 5:3–5. Summarize the attitude toward suffering that we can have through Christ.

God is in control of our lives. Comfort for the dying and their loved ones comes from the God of grace. We rejoice knowing that in our dying, God's Word declares that we are new creatures in the resurrected Christ. "If a man dies, will he live again?" (Job 14:14). Job says: "And after my skin has been destroyed, yet in my flesh I will see God; I myself will see Him with my own eyes—I, and not another. How my heart yearns within me" (Job 19:26–27).

Holy Baptism states that our identity is in Christ. Since we have been baptized into His death and resurrection, we too live a new life in Christ (Romans 6:4). Comfort care begins with the cross of Jesus Christ and continues throughout our earthly life until we stand before the Lord in our heavenly home. "Cast your care on the Lord and He will sustain you; He will never let the righteous fall" (Psalm 55:22).

76. Read John 3:3–5 and Titus 3:5–7. What meaning does Baptism have for end of life situations?

Words
to Remember

B e faithful, even to the point of death, and I will give you the crown of life. Revelation 2:10

Leader Notes

Leaders, please note the different abilities of your class members. Some will easily find Bible passages and pronounce the terms used in this study. Others will struggle. To make participation easier, team up members of the class. For example, if a question asks you to look up several passages, assign one passage to one group, the second to another, and so on. Divide up the work! Let participants present the different answers that they discover. Also, have students turn to the glossary at the back of this book for help with technical terms.

Each topic is divided into four sections:

Focus introduces the topic for discussion.

Science critique summarizes what modern science has discovered about the topic.

Law critique considers the topic in view of God's commands.

Gospel affirmation helps students understand how God addresses the issues raised by the topic through His Son, Jesus Christ.

CHAPTER ONE

And You'll Be Like God

Objectives:

By the power of the Holy Spirit working through God's Word, participants will view 21st-century biotechnology in relation to God's Word; review the Christian's dependence on God; and understand that while all things may be possible, not all things are permissible.

1. Answers will vary. This study will evaluate some of the procedures mentioned by participants.

2. In both cases, the "fruit" is within the grasp of humans, and they imagine that it holds boundless potential for them, godlike potential. Scholars have noted that another way to translate "the tree of the knowledge of good and evil" is "the tree by which good and evil are known." In other words, God set up the tree to be a moral boundary marker. It was good to eat the fruit of the other trees in the garden, but evil to eat from this tree.

3. Solomon addresses this issue more than once. Good intentions are important, but they cannot safeguard against evil. As an English proverb warns, "The road to hell is paved with good intentions." Mary and John need a clear understanding of right and wrong from the Lord.

4. Answers will vary. ART is the work of specialists. The techniques listed in the second paragraph are used at many reproductive clinics.

5. Avoid discussing the decisions of particular people, and answer these questions generally. When technology is used well, the results can be a great blessing.

6. Answers will vary. Let students propose different scenarios.

7. Answers will vary. An infertile couple may turn to ART to overcome their feelings of disappointment or to meet expectations about having children. The drive to have children may so possess them that they may neglect options like adoption.

8. The builders of Babel laid the foundation of their tower and city in human pride. They ignored God's command to "fill and subdue the earth" and instead sought to conquer heaven. Humankind was "playing God."

9. Here God commands the use of technology to save Noah, his family, and the animals. Remember, God is not opposed to technology. He wants us to use technology for His purposes rather than for our own sinful purposes.

10. Adam and Eve intentionally elevated themselves to God's level, overruling His Word about what was right and wrong. Through a lie, Satan also passed judgment on God's Word and His intentions.

"Playing God" is nothing new. Examine the Lord's words to Adam before and after the fall (Genesis 2:8–9; 3). "Playing God" has its roots in Adam and Eve's fall into sin through the deceptive half-truths of Satan. Commanded by the Lord, Adam and Eve were not to eat of the tree of knowing good and evil or they would die a physical death and be separated from Yahweh. Satan tempted Eve with these words: "Did God really say . . . ? You will not surely die. . . . God knows that when you eat of [the fruit] your eyes will be opened, and you will be like God, knowing good and evil" (Genesis 3:1, 4–5).

11. When people put their trust in technology or those who develop technology, they may forget that life truly depends on God rather than man. Science as savior is one of the sins of modern life.

12. God calls parents not just to create life but to nurture and sustain it through His Word. If parents abandon the standards of God's Word in order to bring forth life—using destructive biotechnology—how will they ever pass along God's standards for their children?

13. He chose us in Christ to make us holy. He adopted us as His children.

14. Answers may vary. We can always be sure of God's ultimate will and purpose for our lives, no matter what loss or disappointment we may face.

15. God's Word directs us to look to Jesus. He is the author of our faith. He will "perfect" or complete us by His grace. When we face suffering, we know that we face it with Him.

16. Trinitarian faith is God's gift through Holy Baptism. It treats all human beings as persons created in the image of God. This faith holds to the words and promises of Christ, who gives to us His undeserved love. This agape love does no harm to its neighbor (Romans 13:8ff). As Christians we are to fear and love God so that we do not hurt or harm our neighbor in his body, but help and support him in every physical need (Luther's Small Catechism, Fifth Commandment). This applies to unborn, newborn, and adult human beings.

In the Beginning God Created

Objectives:

B y the power of the Holy Spirit working through God's Word, participants will reaffirm the sanctity of human life through the death and resurrection of Jesus Christ; that a human being's life begins at conception; and that trinitarian faith cares for all human beings as persons created in the image and likeness of God.

17. There is no comparison. David writes in awe of the reproductive process designed by the heavenly Father. Joan, in her zeal to have a healthy child, distances herself from the process.

18. They might argue that cystic fibrosis is a terrible disease and that any loving parent would spare a child from such suffering.

19. This is a central ethical issue for ART. Let participants propose different views freely.

20. A scientist might argue that an amoeba has reached the fullness of its development whereas an embryo is only at the beginning of this process.

21. Everything needed to mature a human being exists at fertilization. From that point on, it is simply a matter of development.

22. Organs used for transplants might be described as "human life" since the cells are human and are alive. But they differ greatly from an embryo, since they have no development as a human being. (The issue of cloning a human being from living human tissue will be addressed in a later session.)

23. Answers will vary. This rule could be used to deny human rights to these groups.

24. As a result of the fall into sin, death has become a consequence of human life from which we cannot escape. The mortality rate of embryos should not become an argument that embryos aren't human. It should remind us of the far-reaching consequences of sin, which corrupts and destroys life at every stage of development.

25. Answers will vary. Note that a human being begins with God, with His handiwork, and not simply the human decision to have sexual intercourse. Truthfully, the wonder of it all is beyond human knowing.

26. Note the words about "life for life." The baby in the womb was regarded as a child.

27. The Bible doesn't permit such a basis for evaluating a human life. Age and development are nonfactors for defining a human being.

28. The terms are "child" and "baby."

29. God views the life in the womb as a child or baby, using the same terms to describe that life after the child is born. This leaves no room for the development argument put forth by some scientists.

30. Although Jesus' conception is very special—that is, by the Holy Spirit—He became like one of us in every way. He passed through all the stages of life—zygotic embryo, embryo, fetus, newborn, child, and adult—so that "He might become a merciful and faithful high priest in service to God, and that He might make atonement for the sins of the people" (Hebrews 2:17).

31. The answer to both questions is conception. Each person begins at conception, not a later stage of development.

32. Jesus didn't treat the human body as an empty shell. He became *man*. The incarnation of Jesus shows how God values you as a person, body and soul. He became like you in every way (yet without sin, Hebrews 4:15), so that He might redeem you in every way.

CHAPTER THREE

In Search of the Perfect Child

Objectives:

By the power of the Holy Spirit working through God's Word, participants will reaffirm God's plan for a one-flesh marriage; review God's Word about procreation, in that children are begotten and not made; review Christian faith and trust in Christ in light of Assisted Reproductive Technology.

33. In the biblical account, Rachel and Leah felt great disgrace when they experienced infertility. Rachel blamed Jacob, and Jacob blamed God. The two sisters even gave their servants to Jacob as surrogates to bear children for him. (This was legal and acceptable at that time in the Middle East.) The entire circumstance caused considerable difficulties for the family.

34. Answers may vary. Clearly God didn't create us for this type of procreation. The thoughtless death of embryos that results from this procedure and the possible complication of family relationships contradicts God's Word.

35. These agreements are custody agreements, just as in a custody battle or an adoption agreement. These agreements suggest that people understand that something far greater than property is involved. Human beings are at stake.

36. This example from the patriarchs reveals the awkward feelings and responses people have under these circumstances. Couples who choose a surrogate birth face considerable difficulties.

37. The loving and caring thing to do in Christ is to leave procreation to the Lord and not to the egg donation of a sister. In addition, this will violate the Ninth and Tenth Commandments regarding seeking what doesn't belong to you, in this case, your sister's eggs or womb. God's Word is clear that the procreation of a child is God's work through the mutual sexual love of a husband and wife (Genesis 1:27–28).

38. Answers will vary.

39. Through prayer and patience, Abram and Sarai have a child. Yet they keep their vows to the Lord. Ultimately, God fulfills His greatest purpose through them: Jesus, the Savior of humanity, is born from their line.

40. St. Paul is seeking that which has been given to him by God's grace through faith—the promise of the resurrection of the body and its union with the soul to live in the eternal blessedness of heaven with Christ. St. Paul knows that by God's grace, heaven is his home now but not yet. Knowing this by faith, Paul continues to pursue this heavenly end in Christ.

41. Of course not. Consider the human desires that Christ experienced growing up in Nazareth. Consider that He was never able to take a wife or have the joy of fatherhood. He knew the ache of empty arms as surely as He knew the pain of pierced hands. You can entrust the future of your marriage and family to Him.

CHAPTER FOUR

The Immortal Clone

Objectives:

By the power of the Holy Spirit working through God's Word, participants will review the basic scientific understanding of human cloning; the role of parenting in seeking to clone a child; and human cloning in light of "serving two masters."

42. Answers will vary. The couple hasn't come to grips with the fact that the cloning of their daughter will result in a different person. Although the child will have the same genetic makeup, the nurture and experience of the child will be different.

43. Answers will vary. Cloning technology is extremely new, but the motives pushing for this technology are not new. The desire for godlike control is almost as old as humanity.

44. Let participants discuss what they know, and then review the facts provided in the student guide.

45. Yes, a clone will be a human being and have a soul. If the answer is "No!" because no sperm are used, then Adam, Eve, and Christ are not human beings with a body and a soul. We know that this isn't true. The more important question is: "What about the salvation of the cloned person?"

46. Answers will vary.

47. Answers will vary.

48. The whole Law shatters. It's like throwing a rock through a window in an attempt to break a small corner. Instead, you shatter the whole window.

49. The following are examples of the uses of eugenics: Between 1927 and 1972 more than 8,000 children and young teenagers were forcibly sterilized at the Lynchburg Colony for the Epileptic and Feebleminded in Virginia. The state claimed that the children had hereditary defects that could potentially be passed on to their off-spring. In fact, the children were simply poor and ill-educated and were considered to be a burden on the state. Today, the Repository for Germinal Choice in Escondido, California, is a eugenic sperm bank that seeks the generation of the most genetically productive people by using sperm donated by persons with a high IQ.

Eugenics marks some people for extinction because they don't measure up to social standards of excellence. The most horrifying example in history is Hitler's Final Solution; his desire to create a strong, healthy, vigorous Aryan people was influenced by U.S. eugenic policy and sterilization laws, which had been declared consti-tutional in 1927.

50. Answers will vary. People with preferred genes would receive preferential treatment. Other people might lose certain rights, undergo sterilization, or even be killed.

51. No. Every person is born sinful and imperfect.

52. The stories tell of the downfall of the strong and the wise. Although physical strength, speed, and genius are blessings, only God can make a person good.

53. Have you ever heard a comedian joke about disciplining a child, "I brought you into this world. And I can take you out!" While this statement is intended to be humorous, imagine the consequences of our throw-away mentality applied to "replaceable" human beings.

54. Cloning holds out false comfort. It can't replace a lost loved one. It can't give immortality. These blessings will only come from God in the resurrection.

55. Answers will vary. In the resurrection, everyone in Christ will be reunited and enjoy the eternal blessings of the Lord in heaven.

The Stem Cell Revolution

Objectives:

By the power of the Holy Spirit working through God's Word, participants will review the basic science of embryonic and adult stem cell sources; review the perils and promises of stem cell research; and reaffirm the sanctity of human life based on God's Word.

56. Answers will vary. Let participants share freely.

57. Cloning embryonic stem cells gives no opportunity for choice to the clones who will be used for therapeutic purposes. The "sacred" will of one person is simply preferred over the will of another.

58. Company A may argue that it doesn't actually destroy the embryos. It simply creates them (like the Bundles of Love Fertility Clinic in the story on p. 15). Company B may argue that these embryos exist anyway; why not put them to therapeutic use? (like the StemCell Bank in the story on p. 41). By dividing the process, the companies seek to escape responsibility while maximizing efficiency and profitability.

59. The Fifth Commandment says: "You will not murder." God forbids us to take the life of another person wrongfully.

The unborn embryo is a human being, created by God to be His own and live under Him in His kingdom. Even if a person clones himself or herself, these clones are human beings who deserve care and nurture with God's means of grace—His Gospel, Holy Baptism, and the Lord's Supper.

60. Adult human cloning violates the First and Fifth Commandments. It uses technology to create an exact copy of yourself, intending either to create a child—which is really your identical twin—or to create an embryonic human being for destruction to recover stem cells that can be used to grow specific cells, tissues, and organs.

61. Just because you have the ability to do something doesn't mean you should use that ability. Adam and Eve had the ability to eat the fruit of the tree of the knowledge of good and evil, yet God specifically told them that it was not theirs to eat. If a soldier has the ability and technology to destroy thousands of human lives, does that mean God wants him to use that ability? Civilization depends on thoughtful restraint of our bodies, wills, and technology.

62. Answers will vary. While some people may restrain their destruction only to embryos, logic will drive many other people to a lack of respect for all human beings. We see this social trend already at work through abortion and euthanasia.

63. Conception can't take place without parents. The embryo can't develop without its mother. A baby depends on its parents/family for food and shelter. Although as adults we may attain considerable independence, a person cannot start a family without another person. In old age a person must depend upon the help of others in order to maintain life. God designed us for caring and mutual interdependence.

64. The Galatians believed they could save themselves through circumcision. Paul warns them that they are trusting in their own works, works that in the end cannot save. True independence/freedom comes through entrusting your life to Christ. Why not let the Maker of heaven and earth, the Savior of the world, bear your burden? Ironically, depending on Christ is the path to genuine independence.

65. Christ freely gave Himself for you. He served you in love by fulfilling the Law of God for your salvation.

66. Answers will vary.

CHAPTER SIX

The Valley of the Shadow of Death

Objectives:

B y the power of the Holy Spirit working through God's Word, participants will reaffirm God's Word on dying well in Christ; the connection between Holy Baptism and dying in Christ; and that we bear each other's burdens.

67. Answers will vary. Some might take these words to mean that it doesn't mater whether we live or die. However, the apostle's point is that no matter what state we are in, we belong to the Lord. We are subject to His Law and are recipients of His blessings in Christ.

68. Durable Power of Attorney (proxy directive) gives authority to a trusted individual to make decisions when a person lapses into incompetence regarding his or her medical care. This provides comfort and direction for loved ones who are entrusted with care and treatment.

69. Certainly not. Though technology has lengthened our lives, it has also prolonged the suffering and isolation of many people. Thank God for technology. But pray that He also grants us greater wisdom in how we use technology.

According to the American Medical Association, persons who are dying need only two things: good symptom control (palliative care) and human presence. The ministry of presence is emphasized by The Lutheran Church—Missouri Synod's Commission on Theology and Church Relations in a publication entitled *Christian Care at Life's End.*

70. Answers will vary. Let participants share their thoughts. Encourage those currently facing difficult situations. Perhaps bring together knowledgeable and experienced people in your congregation to answer questions and offer support to those who are struggling.

71. Wisdom can help us recognize when it's appropriate to let a body rest from treatment.

72. Paul describes death as an enemy. This is certainly true. We shouldn't "make our peace with death." Instead, as Christians, God calls us to make our peace with Him (Isaiah 27:5). More pointedly, He calls us to receive His peace offered through the life, death, and resurrection of His Son. For those in Christ, death is a defeated enemy and eternal life is their hope and blessing.

73. Be sure participants don't receive this passage fatalistically (as though whatever happens is God's will). God permits us to make decisions, even life-and-death decisions. However, as our Maker and Judge, He has the power to overrule our decisions. Life and death ultimately belong to Him.

74. If a participant has a KVJ translation, ask him or her to read this passage aloud. God created us not just "by His will" but "on account of His will." He desires to be with us and enjoy our fellowship.

75. Remarkably, Paul says that we can rejoice in our suffering. This is not meant sadistically. We can rejoice because we know that our suffering is not the end for which God created us. He will sustain us in the midst of it so that we may partake of all He has for us in Christ.

76. Whether one is baptized as an infant or later in life, Baptism works forgiveness of sins, rescues from death and the devil, and gives eternal salvation to all who believe this, as the words and promises of God declare (Romans 5:1–14; 1 Peter 3:21). Baptized Christians know that God calls them His children and that they are not alone, but that Christ walks with them, bringing the hope that is in Him. Baptism tells us that we are in Christ and that physical death is a gain.

These articles were written by Robert Weise for *Bioethics and Faith: Christian Reflections in Health Care and Family Issues,* vol. 1, no. 2 (1999).

The Shadow of Babel

Biotechnology has some people concerned that society is creating a modern Tower of Babel, that is, using technology not only for personal financial gain but also for control and power over nature. This power, like Babel, could possibly lead to greater chaos.

Sir David Lindsey expressed this same concern as far back as 1558, when he wrote in his commentary *Ane Dialog* (First Dialog) regarding the Tower of Babel: "That when the sun is at the height, at noon when it doth shine more bright, the Shadow of that *Hideous Strength* [emphasis added], six miles and more did shoot in length. Thus may you see and judge thereto if Babylon be yes or no" (pp. 24–26). The shadow presents itself as a diabolical chaos that is an extension of man's desire to seek control over self, others, and nature.

This is the origin of C. S. Lewis's book *That Hideous Strength.* In this book he continues his theme of "Man's power over Nature" (p. 67), which he foreshadows in a previous book, *The Abolition of Man.* In both books, he expresses a dire concern for those who seek to exert power and control over nature and people. Herein, the idolatry of humankind expresses itself in those who would lift up technology above the "fear, love, and trust in God above all things."

Yet we live in a world where biotechnology has moved from fiction to fact, especially in the areas of genetics and assisted reproduction. We no longer read and talk about made-to-order babies; we order them. We no longer talk about treating genetic disorders; we use gene replacement therapy. We no longer talk about mapping the human genetic material; we map and identify genes as fast as they are exposed. We no longer talk about living longer; we live longer and look younger. The shadow of biotechnology is "six miles and more."

Therefore, is biotechnology that "hideous strength" which Lewis presents as "the man [who] will not die, the artificial man, free from Nature" (*That Hideous Strength,* p. 177)? Has biotechnology become "that hideous strength," extending its shadow beyond the boundaries of appropriate use to the abyss of human control and power?

Technology is neither value-neutral nor value-free. Jeremy Rifken states in his book *The Biotech Century* that technology is an amplification and extension of our biological bodies. For example, the use of assisted reproductive technologies by infertile couples is merely an extension and amplification of a couple's desire to have a child. He says, "Every tool we've ever created represents increments of power, a way to exercise an advantage over the forces of nature and each other" (p. 288).

Redeemed Christians have freedom within the Gospel of Jesus Christ to use technology in service to God and neighbor. Because Christians are justified (forgiven) by God, "we should fear and love God that we do not hurt or harm our neighbor in his body, but help and support him in every physical need" (the explanation of the Fifth Commandment, Luther's Small Catechism). Our neighbor is the unborn, the newborn, the teenager, the middle-aged, and the older adult.

Following from this presupposition, the responsibility and appropriate use of technology is paramount. This approach will not always provide us with a fail-safe answer in our struggles as new creations in Christ to know with absolute clarity whether or not the use of a specific technology is God-pleasing. And, yes, we could be wrong in our decision to use or not use a specific technology. However, perhaps this approach will provide Christians with an arena to discuss, debate, and prayerfully consider the appropriate use of biotechnology so that "whatever you do, whether in word or deed, do it all in the name of the Lord Jesus, giving thanks to God the Father through Him" (Colossians 3:17).

Bioethics and the Use of the Small and Large Catechisms

Bioethical issues are familiar to most Christians. Few of us are free of the frustration, bewilderment, and consternation over elective abortion, euthanasia, the withholding or withdrawing of a feeding tube, genetic manipulation, organ transplantation, stem cell research, infertility, and cloning. Christian pastors and laity are looking for guidance in these areas so that the Gospel of Jesus Christ is not compromised.

We need to zoom in on the basics of Lutheran Christian education: the Large and Small Catechisms of Pastor Martin Luther. They provide a rich source for approaching bioethical dilemmas in the life and conduct of a Christian. A return to the basics of both catechisms is paramount. Dr. Charles Arand, associate professor of systematic theology at Concordia Seminary, writes: "Basics are those things so foundational that they endure and last in a world where knowledge is ephemeral and fleeting. . . . Basics provide some reference points or set up markers by which we can find our bearings. . . . The catechism fastens our attention on what is most important so that we are not distracted by peripheral issues or concerns" ("Meeting the Challenge for Tomorrow: Formation through Catechesis" in *Formation in the Faith: Catechesis for Tomorrow,* no. 7 [Concordia Seminary Publications, Symposium Papers, 1997], pp. 52–53).

Luther himself suggests the importance of adhering to the basics: "Yet I do as a child who is being taught the Catechism. Every morning, and whenever else I have time, I read and recite word for word the Lord's Prayer, the Ten Commandments, the Creed, the Psalms, etc. I must still read and study the Catechism daily, . . . but I must remain a child and pupil of the Catechism, and I do it gladly"

("Martin Luther's Preface." in the Large Catechism in the *Book of Concord,* Tappert ed., pp. 357–9). One is never too old nor too smart nor too young to return to the basics of Christian Lutheran teachings and faith.

However, the catechisms are not intended to provide Christians a "Betty Crocker cookbook" approach to Christian living. It is not a "how to" book. It is an instructional tool grounded in the Gospel, the Word, and the Sacraments (Holy Baptism and Holy Communion) for "children and uneducated people" that they may grow in grace and knowledge of Jesus Christ. They are a true exposition of the sacred Scriptures because they agree with them and, therefore, are pertinent to Christian conduct and moral judgment.

The basics of catechetical instruction for approaching bioethical issues may begin with the Third Article of the Apostles' Creed—the Gospel of Baptism. God through Baptism gives us our Christian identity. "Baptism signifies . . . why God ordained just this sign and external observance for the Sacrament by which we are first received into the Christian church" ("Baptism" in the Large Catechism in the *Book of Concord,* Tappert ed., pp. 444, 464).

Through Baptism, the Spirit of God brings the Christian to the Creator, "I am the Lord your God," in the First Article and to Jesus Christ, our Redeemer, in the Second Article. Herein, by the creedal Gospel we know that our Christian identity is based on what we have been given by the Lord Jesus Christ who has brought us back from "the devil to God, from death to life, from sin to righteousness, and now keeps us safe there" ("Second Part: The Creed" in the Large Catechism in the *Book of Concord,* Tappert ed., p. 414). This baptismal Christian identity rests in the community of believers, the body of Christ. Therefore, since we are justified by God, we witness the Christ in our doing (or not doing), our speaking, and our thinking to all people around us.

In the Sacrament of the Altar, we receive the "true body and blood of our Lord Jesus Christ, under the bread and wine" ("The Sacrament of the Altar" in the Large Catechism in the *Book of Concord,* Tappert ed., p. 351) "as a pure, wholesome, soothing medicine that aids and quickens us in both soul and body. For where the soul is healed, the body has benefited also" (Ibid., p. 454). It brings strength and nourishment to our body and faith, assuring us not only that our sins are forgiven but also that salvation and eternal life are ours.

Since the catechisms "set forth some key principles for the pastor who wishes to teach the truths of the faith to his people" (A. L. Barry, *What Does This Mean?*: *Catechesis in the Lutheran Congregation,* [CPH, 1996], p. 24), we can use the Small and Large Catechisms to instruct and teach God's people to use God's Word over pious opinion and personal bias. For example, while assisted reproductive technologies may be viewed as adiaphora, that is, provisionally neutral, we could turn to the Fifth Commandment and its explanation: "Thou shalt not kill. *What does this mean?* We should fear and love God so that we do not hurt nor harm our neighbor in his body, but help and support him in every physical need" (*Luther's Small Catechism with Explanation,* p. 10). Because we are Christians with a God-given identity in Christ "who purchased and won me from all sins, from death, and from the power of the devil," we love and serve God and our neighbor as ourself. Therefore, we do no harm to our neighbor, including the smallest of our neighbors: the unborn child. And when this child is born, we bring this child into God's family of grace through Holy Baptism. This approach may be applied to euthanasia, assisted suicide, or any technology that is lifted above the Lord and used as an idol.

Likewise, I would submit that any person who accepts either money for human eggs or sperm or seeks the use of another's sperm, eggs, or womb to bear a child violates the Tenth Commandment: "Thou shalt not covet thy neighbor's wife, nor his manservant, nor his maidservant, nor his cattle, nor anything that is thy neighbor's. *What does this mean?* We should fear and love God so that we do not entice or force away from our neighbor his wife, workers, or animals, or turn them against him, but urge them to stay and do their duty" (*Luther's Small Catechism with Explanation,* p. 11). Ultimately, all abuses of technology take us back to the First Commandment: "Thou shalt have no other gods before Me" (Ibid., p. 9).

Dr. Arand writes, "The analogy of the catechism as a road map to the Christian faith and life might help here. First, a map orients a traveler by marking the major land forms of an area, the coasts, . . . and bodies of water. In a similar way, the catechism orients the Christian by marking our major texts, themes, and events of the Christian life. . . . [It] shows us the contours, features, and characteristics of the Christian life" ("Meeting the Challenge for Tomorrow: Formation through Catechesis" in *Formation in the Faith: Catechesis for Tomorrow,* no. 7 [Concordia Seminary Publications, Symposium Papers, 1997], p. 72).

There are times when we don't know what to do. Likewise, we may be wrong in the final decision. The catechisms are not legal pads of instructions or a fix-all for all bioethical dilemmas. The catechism should not be fragmented or compartmentalized to fit certain situations, but rather should be taken as a whole (the road map analogy), for all of its contents teach us that Jesus Christ is the Way, the Truth, and the Life for Christian living in the twenty-first century.

Glossary

Artificial insemination	The introduction of sperm into the vagina other than by coitus.
Assisted Reproductive Technology (ART)	Technological or medical procedures that assist a man and a woman in reproducing a child other than by coitus.
Adult stem cells (ASC)	Cells found in adult tissues, such as bone marrow, lung, pancreas, brain, breast, fat, and skin (also in umbilical cord and placenta), that contain cells that will develop into tissues or organs.
Cloning	The asexual production of an organism that has an identical genetic constitution to its "parent."
Direct egg sperm injection	Introduction by injection of one sperm into one egg.
Embryo	The developing human from fertilization through the eighth week.
Embryonic stem cells (ESC)	The inner cell mass of a five- to seven-day-old embryonic human being that is harvested, thereby destroying the embryo's life.

Eugenics A science that seeks to improve the hereditary traits of a race or breed.

Gamete intrafallopian transfer The placement of one to three eggs and sperm in a woman's fallopian tubes, attempting to mimic the normal physiological process.

Gospel The message of Christ's death and resurrection for the forgiveness of sins. The Holy Spirit works through the Gospel to create faith and convert people.

In vitro fertilization The process by which an egg and a sperm are combined in a petri dish in an effort to induce fertilization.

Law God's will, which shows people how they should live (e.g., the Ten Commandments) and condemns their failure. The preaching of the Law is the cause of contrition.

Palliative care Proactive, intensive comfort care.

Reproductive cloning Using cloning technology to produce a full-gestational-term cloned human being at birth.

Sentience Awareness of one's surroundings; capable of sensation.

Stem cells Cells that have the ability to divide indefinitely and to give rise to specialized cells (bone marrow, pancreas, skin, muscle, etc.) as well as to produce new stem cells with identical potential.

Therapeutic cloning Using cloning technology to recover cloned embryonic stem cells. One of the main purposes of this approach is to avoid tissue and organ rejection.

Zygote A cell that results from the union of an ocoyte (egg) and a sperm. According to K. L. Moore and T. V. N. Persaud in *The Developing Human: Clinically Oriented Embryology* (1998), "A zygote is the beginning of a new human being."